Too Young to Forget
Poems 1998 - 2010

Philip Burton

Brookware
Printed by Kershaw Print

Published by brookware
2 Foxdale Close
Bacup
Lancs

Tel: 01706 876089
Email: burtophil@hotmail.com
Website: www.philipburton.net

ISBN 978-1-904124-12-2

Printed by Kershaw Print Limited, 928 Burnley Road,
Rossendale, Lancashire, BB4 8QL

Painting *Poppies in the Estuary* by Lynn Bushell

ACKNOWLEDGEMENTS

I dedicate this book to my family and to those who have inspired with the poetry of their lives and works: Lynn Bushell, my tutor Copland Smith, Anne Ryland, and D.A. Prince.

P.N. Review included A Word to the Unwise and Come Day Crow Day in Issue 130. Stand, volume 5 (2) published The Eviction, From The Calm Sea, and Antrin Lichtnin. The Frogmore Papers published Pendle Heritage in September 2001, # 58. Smiths Knoll published dear life in # 38, 2006. The London Magazine included Talking through the top of a glass hat, # April/May 2008. The Royal Festival Hall, Dunsop Valley Spell, and flower of chivalry, are published in The David Jones Journal # 2008.

Thanks are due to the editors of the above, and to editors of the following, where poems in this book, or earlier versions of them, first appeared:

Aabye; Borderlines; Brando's Hat; Breathe; Clitheroe Books Press; Clitheroe Writers Group anthologies; Dawntreader; Dream Catcher; Eclipse; Envoi; Fife Lines; FuseLit; Gentle Reader; Iota poetry quarterly; Konfluence; Links; 2010 Living Word Walks in St Austell and Truro; Magma; Manifold; New Hope International; Orbis; Other Poetry; Parnassus Literary Journal, Georgia USA; Peace Poems (Crocus Books, 2002); Pennine Ink; Poetry Cornwall; poetry monthly; Poetry Now; Poetry Nottingham (eighteen poems in all); Poetry Scotland; Prism International, Canada; Quattrocento; Rain Dog; Sarasvati Literary Magazine; Seam; Skald; Teaspoon Books (2011); The Affectionate Punch; The Brobdignagian Times, Cork; The Coffee House; David Jones Journal; The Piedmont Literary Review, Santa Cruz, California; The Swansea Review; and Weyfarers.

Ship of Rules was a winner of the Lancaster Litfest Poetry Competition in 2005.

The Pocket Watch was short-listed for The Kent and Sussex Open Poetry Competition in 1998, and The Roost received a commendation in 2009. Blessed-fair Sonnet won the Hammicks National Poetry Day Prize, Liverpool in 2002. Holy at Home was short-listed for the Manchester Cathedral International Poetry Competition 2003 and was published in the anthology Taste, published by The University of Central Lancashire, in 2006. The Poetry Shed was short-listed for the Davoren Hanna Poetry Competition in 2004. The Knave's Grave won second prize in the ManyHands Café Poetry Competition, Winter 2009.

The anthology Passing Clouds, Big Lamp Books, 2000, includes Pendle Heritage and The High Road. Blue Grass Blues, Too Young to Forget and Men in Black are included in the anthology Peace Poems, Commonword/Crocus Books, 2003. Antrin Lichtnin is included on a CD, Falling, published by Ann Wilson, in Barrow. Trick of Light is in the anthology Only Connect, Cinnamon Press, 2007. Maps was included in the 2010 Living Word Walks in St Austell and Truro.

Some of these poems appear in poetry pamphlets. The Raven's Diary, was published by joe publish, Project 101, Haslingden,1998. Another pamphlet, Couples, was published by Roundstone Books, Clitheroe, 2008.

Thanks go to Theresa Robson, Jo Harding and all at Pennine Lancashire Poetry Stanza, and to Clitheroe Writers Group for their inspiration and help.

Thanks also to Pennine Ink for reading and checking the text so closely and well.

CONTENTS

NURTURE
DEAR LIFE   1
HEAD OF THE RIVER   2
A LAD'S ESTATE   3
FAMILY GETAWAY   4
GRASS OF PARNASSUS   5
THE FLYING COAT   6
CRACKING PAPER   7
TOWARDS MARS   8
THE ROYAL FESTIVAL HALL   9
GOOD NIGHT TO MY 1951 ROOM   10
BIKING MAD   11
DOWN TO PARADISE   12
RAMSGATE EAST CLIFF SONG   13
RUBY   14
THE POCKET WATCH   15
THE TWILIT ROOM   16
THE DRY SPELL   17
ONE   18
DEAR ANNE   19
READY FOR THE SHOW   20
ON SNOW   21
DROPPING YOU OFF   22

NATURE
THIS PLACE...   23
THE ALLOTMENT CHAIR   24
BLUE GRASS BLUES   25
THE SAND GARDEN   26
PENDLE HAY RIDE   27
DUNSOP VALLEY SPELL   28
THE ROOST   29
SMUGGLED COLOUR   30
GROOSH DITCH RIDDLE   31
THE NEW OASIS   31
DRABA   32
FORBIDDING PASTURE   33
DRY-STONE SKETCH   34

ODE TO SHEEP 35
THE HIGH ROAD 36
SKYLARK 37
THE BRAVE BLACKBIRD 38
ANTRIN LICHTNIN 39
GUEST WORKER 40
LATE AUTUMN WHISPERS 41
THE BLIND ELEPHANT 42
VILLAGE CELESTE 43
A PINE FOREST FIRE 44

NECTAR
PICKLED GHERKINS 45
CLOVE 46
A POSTCARD TO A BAKER 47
THE PIZZA MAN 47

NEAR NAUTICAL
THE GOLDEN CAGE 48
TRYST 49
BRACHYURA 50
SHIP OF RULES 51
...FROM THE CALM SEA 52
SEA VIEWS 53
WITH A NOD TO BEACHY HEAD 54
SPIRIT OF BOSCASTLE 55
BANDSTAND 55
THE LAST RESORT 56
TRICK OF LIGHT 57
LEOPARD COVE 58
SCOTLAND THE BRAVE 59
DOUBLE TAKE 60
WHEN BONFIRES WERE GOLD 61
BEFORE THE STORM 62
TWIN SET 63

NUMINOUS
COME DAY CROW DAY 64
THE PRIZE 65
PENDLE HERITAGE 66
IN THE CHEQUERED ZONE 67
MOUNTAIN STARS 68

HOW DO I LOOK? 69
HIGH CULTURE 69
UNDER WRAPS 70
GABARDINE HUNT OF THE SUN 71
BLESSED-FAIR SONNET 72
MOON DAY 73
THE POETRY SHED 74

NAMELESS
HEALED BY A WORD 75
THE CHEMISTRY BETWEEN 75
THINKING IT A TOY 76
TALKING THROUGH THE TOP OF A GLASS HAT 77
THE BIRTH OF A SPOON 78
THE OPAQUE SPIRIT 79
SACRED MIRROR 80
TELEGRAM 81
MARY YOUNG 82
THE KNAVE'S GRAVE 83
THE MASON'S BRACKET 84
VAN GOGH WAS HERE.... 85
MAPS 86
THE PALM HOUSE OF THE FIVE WINDS, HAIFA 86
SLOE TRAIN 87
PISUM SONG 88
A WORD TO THE UNWISE 89
BEARDED 90
FRANKINCENSE 91
SHOPPING FOR ENGLAND 92
THE BODY OF WORK 93
VESTIGE 93

NARRATIVE
HOLY AT HOME 94
THE SLEEPING WALK TO PELEKAS 95

NEMESIS
FLOWER OF CHIVALRY 97
JUDITH 98
A LOWRY 99
THE FUNERAL OF MY AUNT 100
THE PASSING ON OF HATS 101

THE PASSING OF A PIPE 102
NEEDLE 103
TOO YOUNG TO FORGET 104
MENIN BLACK 105
I'LL WAIT HERE 106
FUNERARY RONDEL 107
THE YOUNG TOMB 108
ST. BEDE THE VENERABLE 109
A VILLANELLE FOR BERNARD 110
RED OCTOBER 111
THE TREES ARE DOWN 112
VILLAGE CELESTE 113
THE EVICTION 114

DEAR LIFE

have you thought lighthouse?
stand for something
for once

or act
the pearly queen of sand -
oyster as your world

or be a dry dock –
a womb-wide
hospital for hulls

or be - that iceberg
of prolonged meditation -
Kontiki

or a little Nautilus
and blend
like a linseed brush

or why not hover –
spend ages
weighing luxury cruises

or shred the catalogue
strip to the buff
risk the rip tide

admit you're
a vestige of the sea -
go - make waves

HEAD OF THE RIVER

Lowgill took me back

Seated near the Bowland brook
teased by runes of wrinkled shade
I was in class again

counted as one to whom no regard
was best given – dyslexic we'd say now,
shiftless then.

Nibs always bent, blots ruled okay.
Because I could not write, my heart hurt;
my backside too.

What saved me at school
were the high windows – square kites -
steadfast blue visited by white.

I understood Kent's River Stour -
sailed my mind's eye along it each day
from Westmarsh to Durnock.

If only they'd ask me to read aloud
its cordovan banks, hump-neck bridges,
slow cursive bends.

Paper words – second nature to my peers –
were rivers too, oxbow islands,
inlets with no landing-stage.

A LAD'S ESTATE

The vehicle sat, one day, soft in the barn,
with whispering craneflies and fat fieldmouse.
Spearmint shafts of sunlight felt us
cowering, thief-thick, quiet.
                          Then, alarm.
Sour tomcats dodged imagined hooves,
weasel cages danced, Barn owls woke.
Calm usual crows exploded
at the motor car ignition. It shook
                  all tongues and grooves.

She'd sleep beneath a canvas
                    that kept the 'hen do' off.
And when we'd growled home
I'd sprawl and hear the secret random
song of cooling body parts, and cough
the petrol asking for my blood.

I'd sneak below the stiff tarpaulin,
taste the shellac varnish of her wing,
climb the ashwood ladder of her side,
lay up on her silken roof.
                    And dream.

FAMILY GETAWAY

I fidgeted all the ditch-long journey
envious of my sister's headlong sleep.
After the wringing-out of sandwiches -
and top-heavy march in heavy top fields

with canvas that had fought at Mons -
we settled on the forest edge
stiff and cold as the pines themselves,
in waterproofs heavy as Cornwall.

I had packed the usual suspects -
dismal diary, bare-spined Dickens,
liquorice lace - to tie the journey's ends.
Sealed against toads, we unfurled

our brief beds, wet in our sacks,
our eyes rainstuck, touching home
by mercy of dreams. Then the going down
for milk, carrying dawn on our backs

through cow pat fields, like sappers.
Then a powwow round the primus
making puddle plans and stroking knees
like poultices, scouting for songs.

Narrow, awake, among the dark
I sensed the dust heart of the conifers.

GRASS OF PARNASSUS

Both wrists in the manacled grip
of a Sunday walk, I seize a slack moment
to fly away like sand from a fist
off down the vale of the dunes.

I taste the worry in one adult voice
but the wind makes words into sun.
The best bellow turns yellow, then beige
in the undulating calm.

The only guidance remaining is silence
drowned by the glare of cumulus clouds.
A tot all at sea in a ballpool
I lie for a while, tickled by round,

bucketless, spade-free, spillable hills
building their warrens and wynds –
a great gold ship with grasses for oars
and beached for a while on a shore like mine.

Between farm and bight I find an anchor
tall as a wish propped up in the clay -
a treat of a buttercup, white, whiter -
misbehaviour gleaming at me.

THE FLYING COAT

we'd loll in the well
of the old wardrobe –
navigator him – pilot me –
on convoy

easy to talk to
terrible to listen to -
my father's leather flying coat
had no more stomach for clouds

teach me how to fly
I'd say, but no sound came -
only the lean whirr of air
fighting for lungs

this was the war my father
brought back, a story
too sick to sit and tell –
his refuelled grief

taking him off
to a distant bed
with earpiece, crystal set
and clouded eyes

CRACKING PAPER

Breakfasting
on others' news -
held high

to barricade
the life
out of us -

allows me
to read the sport -
its disciplines.

You live
front to back
with crime.

You live
with raised fists
and low heart.

You fight
to sit still for it.
Can't you see?

TOWARDS MARS

If you find yourself drawn-up towards the planet (Mars),
you will develop keen judgement ...

\- The Wordsworth Dictionary of Dreams
        Gustavus Hindman Miller

My father was clear - my binoculars
should be cleaned, polished, cased,
and some distant day I'd grow into them.

But, when night was lit by a million stars
I'd shadow the shadows down the hall
turn the loose key. Slow as moons wax

I'd release them - all their X10 power
angled across an open Biggles book
at my bedservatory window.

Mars can appear a red quivering marble
or a cotton pad where a nose has bled
or a button scratched by sandy beaches

until thin gone. But one time Mars grew
and grew, and I went on a journey.
The pull of Space possessed me.

Mars drew me up to its full height.
Who can I tell? I'd be laughed out of sight.
Some day they'll grow into it.

THE ROYAL FESTIVAL HALL

This festival is Britain, she said,
or the best of it, what remains.

And will there be horses and red
queens, and bob-nosed clowns
and cherries for sale or free
and a chatty face in a gypsy tent?

And all these were there, and trees
as tall as canes, and young men
with barracking strides, worn
eyes, and still wet wounds.
And sky was brought indoors
and beat with a drum of sound.

This was Royal and Festival
and Hall rolled into one,
swelling with each new arrival
and every Briton must have come.

Stairs went up for ever more.
Like spitfire trails, we dizzied
looking from the second floor
tasting the way pilots lived.

'The Skylon' pointing off
to other worlds - one high
the other low – made us laugh.
1951. We'd come through.

GOOD NIGHT TO MY 1951 ROOM

Lace on the sills, linoleum floor,
newsprint informing the chest of drawers:
candlewick straining the trestle bed:
tallboy glowing with beeswax ease:
floorboards to filter the wind's groans:
apple box ripe with lathe-turned toys –

diablo, skittles, whipping tops, and pawns:
orange box of racing cars in racing green,
custard yellow, bluebell blue, and snow:
a loosely leaning crane of shot Meccano:
gold framed granddad lost in amber
having his smile become my own:

the slow march of ocean by the window:
the clock forever stopped, the curtain torn:
ancient roses letting their perfume flow
till it spills across my yawn:
and Mother putting her head round the door.
Where are they now these things I own?

BIKING MAD

Gliding along, with her half-hitched-up skirt,
my aunt was a better cyclist than me.
I couldn't keep up. I suffered a hurt -
a jolt to my young masculinity.

My aunt was a better cyclist than me;
elegant, fast, and - I underline -
a jolt to my young masculinity.
If she were unstable, I saw no sign.

Elegant, fast, and - I underline -
she made enemies in our blokish town.
If she were unstable, I saw no sign.
I dropped off the pace, with a teenage frown.

She made enemies in our blokish town
idle tongues would say she could ill-afford.
I dropped off the pace, with a teenage frown.
They wheeled her away, to a mental ward.

Idle tongues would say she could ill-afford
gliding along with her half-hitched-up skirt.
They wheeled her away, to a mental ward.
I couldn't keep up. I suffered a hurt.

DOWN TO PARADISE

Under the low highway lies a pitiless
echo-bound way turning out trodden things
tossed wrappers and wretched emptiness.
A dear child, echoing mother's mood-swing
chances a laugh. The stone-lipped sourness
of tunnel sucks in and invents a clever opening
and the grey crocked tiles retire in backness.
Seagulls dip suddenly, sloping a wing.

The disturbed ocean's stereo-confessions cease.
The stained flags of foot ache concrete fall away
into the shoe-deep sand's gold-grained caress.
Miracles perform within the child's play
to rock the shelvy porcelain sea's vastness.
Darting to fill a pail of spray
to bring lightness to Mother with such fine finesse
he marks a turning point, a fulfilling.

RAMSGATE, EAST CLIFF SONG

We approach from the brick butt Regency back-street.
A roped song, of rain, fog, and salt, climbs the stacks.
An old buck's pantaloons flap Calais-wards
held by a whisker of twisted peg

to a ringlet balcony. Marge is on the piano
and the pub door creaks a tuba part, very discreet.
There's a debate. She wins with,

Let's go melt the tongue of November on a lungful of coffee.
It's a long puddle up from the sea.
The ocean looks flat from here.
The cliff rules. Above its white cavity, a gull wheels.

The café's side window, partly steamed,
is a view through the front glass to the peeling clouds
and the kissed girl running for cover
ribbon blown loose as the sea's mystery.

RUBY

for Nadie

her clock had been genteel
like her, and broken

I farmed, in my treasure tin
each fretted wheel
each fiddly token

and her spirit in the thing –
a red sealed
world, soft spoken
as a camera winding

I sought the ruby out the other day
among playing cards,
wrinkled acorns, bits of clay

and it winked at me hard
again, in that same asterismic way

THE POCKET WATCH

Grandad improved it? The mottle glares. Lion
that he was, the veins must end. Gold, brass, iron -
licked undone by loose chain, bus-driver serge,
crocus powder, emery, steel wool and rouge.
But spring open! Delve below spoiled crystal;

he smoothed the bevels, scraped burr and embossed
an escape of creamed precision. He hatched and crossed
the haloed pendant; no ear lobe silkier!
Metal fragments? All eliminated. Sheer
graft, anointed with oil, with turpentine.

Gold ovoid nestles, beating, on my palm,
mainspring hidden deep in vinegary charm.
Self-referential galaxy of ramshackle-hung
precise wheels pricked by arbors of steel, sprung
like velitating pixies on pressed jewels!

THE TWILIT ROOM

The bell-push repels. You would never have one.
Or that prissy window box with gentians.
And your twilit room, what is it like thirty years on?
Not a decent plan to knock and ask, "Could you
arrange for me? You knew my gran?
Bright as yellow gloves, in her mauve cardigan."
You had kept them all out - Fritz, burglars, taxmen.
Retained your chestnut wall, that gingham cage,
the cobaltic glass swan, Degas: Awaiting the cue.

They have sanded the façade. Men deranged
with masks, and dinning hi-fi, sealed the bricks
that once had steamed with many-crated scents.
Even now you might, a hatpin away, lever-back
the bent lace. Your face understood wars -
bested whatever they sent against you.

THE DRY SPELL

Such white that year! Chalk breeze
dimmed the cat's-eyes road, the trees,
speckled the wrens' eggs, dusted the field,
rotted each stitch in the canvas marquee.

We'd people to go, placements to be,
those dread digs and University.
We stowed the kit and kissed the crease
and promised that we'd often meet.

Whiter than the ancient screen
the pitch held footprints hornblende green
dry as any grass has been,
drier than dreams, than fresh green

departing men, or angels suddenly,
lifted by the moment, shaken free
of close friends, already empty,
eyes made white by lightning sheets.

White water canvassed down between
the lost pavilion's creaking seams
bowling-out the pastel scene
knocking the bails off our late teens.

In winter snow I often dream,
transported to those white streams
that downed the tent in that white field,
when I was young and at my ease.

ONE

Schooled at Sherborne, One tried to put a curb on
me North, or, as he would prefer, mouth.

I wondered why One one'd. I's tightly shunned.
Different source, old boy. Yours? H.P.? Mine? Soy.

My o's were solid ow's. We came to blows, had rows.
I started dropping h's that/which I hadn't done for ages.

I taught One to spit. One taught me that caps fit
but blokes don't need to, and how to practically joke.

He became a real bruv, but died behind the wheel
in his Mini van phase. One did in those days.

DEAR ANNE, *for Anne Ryland*

Thank you for the lovely poems.
Thank goodness

I never had the chance to spoil you.
If I had been your teacher

and it became apparent that you
were my new class chatterbox

I would have quelled you
                – best of intentions -

the science did not, then, exist
that tells us jaw jaw
betters the raw score

or, to blather gathers
while shtum stays dumb

I would have shut your chatter
in the box of your fond mind

with the zest of intentions
and scholar'd you with quiet

and you would have belled
and rebelled and turned

motley as an old draughts board.
You would still have queen'd

because of the words in you

READY FOR THE SHOW

The house was like an auction or a fair
until the lot of us were safe in bed.
                          - Charlotte Mew: The Quiet House

I, hammering away at la Bruyere.
You round me. Witches from Macbeth
never in a line, tripping on spills of toys.
"This doll is the wicker queen. This."
"No, have one who squeaks evil noises."
The play, like a ghost train, couldn't miss.

Five full faces, bidding for an audience.
"Five minutes. Less. Four. Or just three."
"So short you'll have it in a sentence."
"Come and watch our puppets, Daddy."

Such intimate theatre. And no two acts
the same. The affecting silences, the shot
glances, the instant re-writes, edits
on the hoof, the ever-stirring pot.

ON SNOW

Jenny quizzed her footprints right and left.
Why are you just like my boots?
And why do you follow me, you pests?
When I run, why do you explode?

What can my snowy footprints tell?
Can we do a science task?
After the ringing of her Nursery bell
the teacher marvelled at what Jenny asked.

Aged twelve, Jen devised an experiment
with a wellington of warm water, to discern
how snow melts, over time, under radiant
heat, creating the tracks of a monster.

At sixteen she made herself think on
how an Alpine valley got too warm
and she tied a hundred pale blue ribbons
to welcome the ice, if ever it return.

Jennifer still questions snow.
"Never crystal clear, but why opaque?
And the fearful crunch boots undergo!
How can you, so soft, mechanically break?"
She is reading science at Birkbeck.

A snowball holds together, that's a mystery
to me, because I studied chemistry.

DROPPING YOU OFF

Together we spruce up your duvet,
kneel and gather your shoes,
leave go in the tunnel of bed
the playful teddies, loyal toys,
deflated wings, lesser diplomas.

We become twins in the car - father
and son watching two birdmen
stride off Bognor Regis pier.
Time flies with brute elegance.
Au revoir mon etudiant.

Rockpools, confounded by surf,
have their brief life sucked away.
The arcade blinks and swallows a cough.
The seafront throbs in neutral.
On to Chichester University.

At Postiche House we hug and part.
On my return to the strandline
I disturb a pale outed sunstar
among the sog, an upper shoe,
bootlace weed Corda filum

long as a Greek shipping route,
and, in a holdfast claw of kelp,
a tiny Porcelain crab - caught -
small as the world it has lost -
not aware it has summoned help.

THIS PLACE DOES NOT SERVE THE EASY

after Dylan Thomas

The path to Fern Hill, part metaphor, part hardcore,
is neglected. Ill elms, pasty in the whispering light,
overwhelm the apple boughs, reinforce the eye-sore.
One glad heron stands, lit by a fanlight
of absent branches, on a pedestal drowned by ferns.
Pinking sounds startle me, an aching caravan returns
up the Saint Clears road. No happy boy. No ghost.

I'll haunt his dog, then (dog his haunt).
                        The pub yard spills redcurrant.
No. Blood-red crates. A shed reads 'vacant'.

Find him at the sea, the curved lanes urge,
and soon the bracket hedge reveals his ocean
cool and clean and cloudy as his verse, rolling
to a second death where Ginst and Wharley merge.

THE ALLOTMENT CHAIR

Jed's plot was a throwback to Eden.
Dog strollers broke stride, workmen softened.
Sunday folk watched him charm turnips
from early winter beds, shake his hips

at girls. And he'd give a deft display
to show that digging's about wrist, and say
that a thousand pounds drive a spade's haft
but a soft forearm and a gentle shove

will turn the clods, even in quagmire.
There was lightness in him; he'd not cease
till catalogues refrained from new varieties.
But the clanging of church spades

told of an elder's death – and it's Jed's turn
to lock horns with the allotment chair,
lend his plot to younger blood, and laze
beneath his laurels, turn seasons into days.

He toys with orchids, cress, Bonsai,
the raking of castrated leaves toward the fire.
But most he sits so long he's taking root
awaiting time and tide like King Canute.

BLUE GRASS BLUES

I'll live in grass that's thistle-blue,
heave buckets to flush the john
watch the wide Missouri
as it ambles broadly on.

I hunger for hootenanny
where night is hot and long
and belt-and-braces canny
men to tell me when I'm wrong.

I hanker for candy-crunch washboards,
and banjos like peppery spoons.
I yearn to roll on cobs of corn
with cousins in tumble-down barns.

I yearn for young Virginia
with a rip in her cargo jeans
a hickory lap-top processor
and her rocking-chair that leans.

I'll live in grass that's thistle-blue,
heave buckets to flush the john
watch the wide Missouri
as it ambles broadly on.

THE SAND GARDEN

I unearthed an edge to the new ground.
Mineral with animal connections:
a gravestone larger than death,
a standing stone grown tired, sunk
back to loamy bed, latent, duvet-deep
for me to find.
                    But rather than disturb
I leave a space in the Escallonia,
welcome the sand as it idles through,
put shallow things here. Radishes.
Driftwood brushed by starlit oceans.
Shells combed pale: Peppery Furrow,
Thin Tellin, Cockle, White Tortoiseshell

insubstantial as the moon

PENDLE HAY RIDE

I'd like to ride on an old farm cart.
I'd lie in the sun and wait for the start.
I'd fall asleep on the spice clean hay.
I'd wake as the driver pulled the rein

to say, Gee up Frankincense!
down the way from Higham to Fence
up the back lane, along the top road
to Old Read, Trapp Forge where we always slowed;
then White Hill, Well Wood, Black Hill,
Chew Barn, Nutter Barn, up past the school,
Pendle Nick, sand pit, and Coffin Stone,
Wymondhouse, Audley, and Cold Coats,

Tarry Barn, Ivy Cott, Standen Hall,
Clitheroe town, our very last call.

DUNSOP VALLEY SPELL

The purple flags of Foxglove
and Creeping Thistles rise to shine
above browbeaten bracken.
A skeleton track tells, in runes,
of high trees brought low.
Soon hillsides will be broadleaved -
smart cash has fled from Pine.

This is shooting-party land.
The needs of Grouse, at any cost
are met. And yet the river
chooses its own bed, and how
the day's Oystercatcher-quarrel
and wind that wings the willow
prick the casual visitor to life.

A vaccary wall's tight stack
of white-watered river stones
holds the past in a sentence line.
Monarchs still come here
making a progress, breathing;
the last to shoot the wildlife
was Richard Coeur de Lion.

THE ROOST

Brookside Nurseries, Rossendale

Rustic, rust free, underblown -
in the way that woodsmen handle the task -
the roofs aren't the usual Toblerones
but reflect the heights and habits of plants.

The freehold is owned by Muscovy ducks
and there's Garden Centre periphery
where the unbilled visitors have to tut
their troubled way through volcanic ferns.

Ah, Pennyroyal's nice, but it soon dies.
Would you say pansies are right for a him?
And where in pots are the Persil fries
that Nan applies to her rheumatism?

Between the Malay terracotta -
can you see, can you see, white and umber,
one eye a Flanders poppy, one not,
a bird on a break from the mud pool?

Did you know they're over from Brazil?
They have this yen, folk there, for soybean.
So she can't roost - habitat if you will.
She's taken off now to the old Ash tree.

You forget that she has the wing-power.
And they all flew last year. To Baxenden.
Licking their long claws, they returned
with a lad in a pantechnicon.

SMUGGLED COLOUR

Sky-dotted Violet cress.
A green tunnel of trees.
The luminous alfalfa seed
bought in bulk for cultivating cattle feed
saying, Don't bury me in soil. Cremate me.
And in among that luzerne
or Provencal glow-worm,
a stowaway, a weed seed
but a very acceptable impurity,
the dull rough marshmallow.
Such a strong stem,
and in the profile of its lobed leaf
a cathedral facade
lit with candles from below.

GROOSH DITCH RIDDLE

Given I haunt the oak litter and barely live at all
How come I'll not stoop to your 'nature reserve'?
Oh, they misnamed me 'coralroot' (spurred,
Spur-lipped). Quite absurd
Though I too feed on the dead.
Oh, I am a genus apart. I've nothing green.
Reflect on my glassy stems.
Call my flower lobster-flesh.
Have you thought my seed rare? As fertile as gems?
I know my seed is everywhere
Daring just rarely to exorcise me.

THE NEW OASIS

The tarmac appears permanent today.
But 'road-metal' is just weakened stone.
Though early sun shines it like a railway
the sub-soil's only marking time below.
On the estate corner churned by streams
of diesels clumping the odd wheel over
I notice for the first time: a fault, a dream
of what was once there: a galaxy of clover
lit by a buttercup supernova.
I walk on hurriedly. The oasis
can't persist for long, won't recover;
one random swerve of an articulated chassis....
Where I turn for home the road swoons
in a cul-de-sac, gives birth to gardens.

DRABA

I like this wildflower's blunt Latin tag:
Draba which, in winter, absolutely fits.
Yet in Spring it's 'Yellow Whitlow-grass'.

Did a botanist walk this coast
one isolated March and think,
"This weed, surely there's none drabber?"

Find this schizonomer only on The Gower
among the fossil bones of white hyena.
Or straying along the cliffwalk walls.

Insular, fending off the eye with lance-
leaves fringed with blanched bristles,
perched on the crumble, neat and stiff

lime drab until an April yellow flower
pitches perfect petals, and from that hour
Draba's gone; there's only Whitlow-grass.

FORBIDDING PASTURE

The field is hemmed by hawthorn
wet stone, and the thin gesture of wire.

Each fresh season I'm drawn
to dig my old bones out of the divan
and ramble the Lottery-funded footpath.

I peer through the padded curtain.
Hot-day gusts pollinate my eyes.
Nettles. Let butterfly men be drawn
I stay and pay the rent or scratch the nose.

September. Cow-pats reek the grass.
Bramble leaders knit a noose.
Or the timbre's wrong. Soon frost
will lock me home, a Jonah with a belly,
and only Mrs Fox will test
the right to roam.

DRY-STONE SKETCH

The dry laugh enshrined in 'dry-stone wall'
takes on an edge, on Todmorden Edge:
the neat castellated touch, the cold breast
of shepherd's hearth, the odd 'pile of stones'
motif. And the wry additions of thrift:
the offcut of drainage pipe, a door brick,
a missing milestone, a fossil bone.

Dry-stone walls, iced through, rear
and slide like lardy shears from corned
hands. Well-straggled stones press on
up the fell to Cliviger Canyon to skirt
Holme Chapel, Bull's Head, Overtown.
Here, flocculent sheep merge with cloud,
lost to their own snow-dusted tracks;

the sheep re-emerge on Thieveley Scout
in April, hard as skin on crab-apple,
survived where grass grinds out a draw.
From here, unmolested, unrepaired,
unmortared stone keeps rough line
Boulsworth Hill to Widdop, Howarth
Moor, the parsonage.

ODE TO SHEEP

I like being ignored by the watchful eye
of a flock of sheep on their daily grind.
What silent airy landscape, almost sky
they nearly inhabit. Where do they find
the stimuli to know they are not dead?

Sun-rich buttercups and pot-hole smells
can only feed a five-minute ecstasy
and yet they look alert and interested.

Perhaps their busy minds store details
for a book 'Grass Management Looks Easy'.

THE HIGH ROAD

no mistake, a sheep on a high stone wall
head lifted, footsure, coping
twelve feet up or more

a ewe glides, rides the updraft
of blackened stone
with solid white force

her perfect lambs, hardly born,
dance to their ewe,
their vagrant saint of lost causeways

round an old coal-yard (now a tip for spoil)
lost in ferns.
Stones lean hard against the sheep-track,

retains the moors, but not the mouflons'
wild impulse-
in one tight flash they're down,

to walk, like road-inspectors, into town

SKYLARK

chanter alouette

swift as old age
skylark died

skylark died -
we are dumb

skylark - Beethoven
high as hot helium

no better call
on people's time -
to hear, above all,
and all day long
skylark song

when skylark lived -
we were deaf
skylark died -
we are dumb

THE BRAVE BLACKBIRD

I admire, through the white-rimmed pane,
the owner of the well-trimmed lawn.
Brave, bull-black, oblique.
His bonus ball of blackberry gone
he tunes to tremors from the catacomb,

feels the trickle of compression
moving out beyond the rising worm.
The blackbird's perfect fulcrum leans
into the first heaving of the storm,
spears his prey, takes up the tension.

The delayed leaves lift from the rowan,
fall as dry rain, covering the blackbird
momentarily. Revealing him again,
a statue in the reliquary garden
dedicated to the tug-o-war.

He blinks his morsel down. And then he's gone.

ANTRIN LICHTNIN

A tame idea to have, that wildlife
would hunker down
and - like model folk in the military town
behind the bridal white
neck of canal –
defer to the veil of spotless rain
soon to hide Ben Bahn,
Ardgour, far away Mull.

But no. Above the scumble of heather -
needling in
on covert wings
like Venus viewed through conifer
a prey bird plummeted
onto cold fallow like a blown kiss -
the great gold nape, apotheosis
of pride.

Then the ruck of talon on fur
pre-chilled in the stubborn glen,
the slow metronomic flap again
of force majeure

then to high Gulvain
through soft confetti Highland rain.

GUEST WORKER

The moon is amplified by sunflowers.
Moon-clouds waver above shadows.
The earth's underarm is sweet. Showers
all day have topped and tailed the meadows
framing the buttery stone of Cheltenham.
Along the oaty-mortar-and-honey walls,
along rebel areas of wild marjoram,
beyond the egg-white gates and lintels
strides the urban fox on his quiet quest.
He yawns in contempt at my mock whistle,
runs to paw the blood-smells, is my guess,
behind the Co-op. Then a black bristle
of garden sweeps him, inheres him.
I turn my collar inside, like one wet ear.

LATE AUTUMN WHISPERS

The fox flares her hungry nose. A speck of red
in the far field. A tired maple. Otiose Autumn.
The bilberry mist has rained its seed. The woods blaze
from shadow, though the funeral pyre's gone.
The fox-trails colden, stifled in lingering smoke.

The snow is slow to come. A shallow breeze
partly from the north, musses its paws
among dead leaves. Everything just exactly so:
corn-meal, strong in the byre: the harvester
greased and under wraps: the dead, quiet.

The lonely cartwheel spins the combing flakes
to brush its lean spokes. Leather straps whip
the alder-pegs on the flapping stable door.
The furrows narrow to a dotted line.
The tired vixen screams, and goes to earth.

The farm lies open as a night before a war.
"I come to you my love, to cover you,"
a whisper made of silence in the coppice,
the only-ever-promise made by new snow.
The grudge-deep ditch fills, is forgotten.

THE BLIND ELEPHANT

blindness spares the elephant
long grey vistas
   of courtyard sealed in concrete;
blindness tunes the elephant
to the heavy aftershave
that brings the vegetable man

she hangs a trunk of gratefulness
   for these, and winds that hose
and the waterhole of sleep returning,
companionable buffets
from elephantine friends,
heat from high summer, cold from low

she is aware of unused rooms
   in the palace of her head,
a thousand trails never to be travelled,
loud shovelling of spoors ahead of her,
and, in her middle ear,
the riddle-cage call of African cats

VILLAGE CELESTE

Roads quarter the common. Evening drags
at dimpled stone. Residual clock-hands
on the tower proclaim that it is midnight
or, if day, noon.

All is closed save the graveyard.
The stock of village life (the pub, the school,
the general store), hollow megaliths
among the solid ripeness of the corn.

Above a lodge a weathervane is bent
immobile, as if one sign of change
would summon Death, disturb the warden.
A window droops in ivy's dull mask.

The wine-cellar door is steeled with nails.
The famous kitchen garden, umber-lit
encroached by pines, shows only remnant
mutant cabbages, and dry cider-traps.

No meadows of tawny, tan and grey;
only standard gold, and modified rape
to come, and the grubbing-machine
in the long hedge of a child's laugh.

A PINE FOREST FIRE

Watch the birdie, darling. Glad we came.
Click click, till a crossbill yips alarm
and three magpies fountain up out.
Everything starts to forget its name:
women, fire, and dangerous things.

On the ripe cones, the rows of scales
are individual blazes - chandeliers
highlighting pins on the floor.
Flame has come as group photographer
giving commands in a crisper voice

for needle hair to be combed straight -
for trunks to flash their highest thighs –
for the bark to bake and peel and smile –
for Holly to raise her leather hands
unclaw her varnished fingernails

and embrace the hot new discipline.
Puffball squirrels, jumpy shadows,
make no apologies to go by meadow
just this once, bounding the tufted grass
as occult shivers of twilight.

PICKLED GHERKINS

My uncle Taddy, from Gdansk
in Poland, loves his pickles.

He would not give a thank you
for fresh stuff. He makes planks -

long strips of pickled gherkin
to cover his plate edge in.

He puts mountains of vinegary
cabbage in the middle like a V

and - in between - a walnut
or two from a jar, like Pizza Hut

and then some Pan Yan
and potato salad if he can.
His plate is full and beautiful
and when he takes a mouthful

my auntie laughs.

CLOVE

Essential Sunday slumps
under a dead hand of steam –
gently returning to dough.
Edging. All that remains.
Neat as a dog collar.
It illustrates the way
all us feasters and fasters

caved in to frozen food.
And now every day is
Regulus Wednesday
yawning its groundhog smile.
Only kitchen basil
plays truant from the over-zealous
hood. No hint of a clove
in an apple pie's heart
licking your nose
like old dog Sunday
attentive to something higher.
Take a sniff at the freezer
And tell me it is not so.

A POSTCARD TO A BAKER

IN A TOWN IN THE SOUTH OF ISRAEL
FEBRUARY 1968

You broke a sweltering baguette
and lay each half on my palms.

My taste of poverty tailed away;
an obscure comet with a slender trace
and the echo of Psalms.
What remains is you blowing your thumb.

THE PIZZA MAN

He struts his stuff
a star commander
armed with epaulettes of sweat.

He flours the air with meteors
flattens his orbs of moon pastry
shuttled between flat hob
and the waggling curvatures of space.

He docks at last
with fragrant anchovies
to set course for the sun

or at least, the oven.

THE GOLDEN CAGE

St Agnes, Cornwall

Hid from the blood cough of the sea
and all its lingering designs -
the nesting thatch of cottages climbs
in tendrils of Russian vine
the anchoring hill toward Goonrea.

St Agnes' folk - so far back then -
thought summer was abducted by
migrating cuckoos, in July,
for use abroad. Not to decry
the logic of these ancients

who noted the lower flight-path -
the way these birds hug the contour
of bush and knoll – and seldom soar
the way that swifts and woodlarks do.
They said, "We shall build a high garth

wall around the village spinney;
summer stays if cuckoos are kept!"
Sure as stranded stacks of kelp
retain sand-flies, and cliffs are left
the ocean's massive dignity

St Agnes catches autumn fast
when all the migrant birds are gone.
Shades of blood, fire, the stones
of towering folly, remind
us that - though summers pass -

mists of autumn seldom clear -
but often shut kind faces down
in drifts, leave   just the ostrich frown
of gulls, off The Head, sifting bones.
And peas that soak, all night, in beer.

TRYST

In the wide sea's molten mind
thoughts re-draft,
ebb, flow, from limpid rivers

deep and far, no word of land
till the ocean sculpts
love letters in Cornwall's coast.

West of Newquay's Watergate
at Lusty Glaze Bay –
"A Place To View Blue Boats"

there is evidence of reply:
cut in the cliff, a steep flight
that - like a stolen heart -

quickens, even as it's lost
under startled falls of shale.
How long since folk made

how desperate a daily trudge
without a railing or a post.
Lower, the riser ghosts
march in their own right
with none but spray and gulls
into the hammer of the waves.

When the sea turns for home,
reduced steps emerge -
an infant slide

a standing wave to Mother.

BRACHYURA

When florist-wire
tightens round my soul
I'll reach for weighted hook and line
I'll kick my feet
glibly off the pier
where silver seagulls pebble-dash
the blank sea wall
I'll settle down to do or drown
where sea and river duel

alone in the dilution zone
a cleft-clever sidling stone
will eyeball
the pencil-sharp intruder

will clamp the bait
be drawn through air
on the bacon strap
the Common crab
will drip dignity

I'll relent and cut the tie

SHIP OF RULES

It isn't a museum, but it's absolutely free.
The turnstile had been a capstan.
He'll insist that visiting hands be clean:
chairs, not to be collapsed on.
There'll be water biscuits with Earl Grey tea
served with a steady hand.

He'll show - balsa hull readied with cement -
how hidden hinges, thread, cans
create a Javanese junco inside a demijohn,
flick the sails to life like oriental fans
each lugsail, each batten - and not one bent.
Admire the deftness of the man.

He's corridors of HMS-this, HMS-the-other.
Every blessed rivet, each god-awful gun.
Every porthole trim as an antiseptic odour.
No acrid smoke. No rum.
No midshipman, drunk. No dyspeptic stoker.
No wit. No quirks. No fun.

This, after all, is his bread and margarine -
but get invited, if you can
to his living room. His heart has been
busier here. All his talent
shines in North Foreland Lightship 1953.
Here, his style meant

rust gets to creep along the black aft bilge.
The rule-book, on the bridge floor
flaps in a Force Nine, page by fogged page.
The First Mate's caught in a roar
for more chain, and the ship's cat waits,
tongue on paw.

...FROM THE CALM SEA

A seal rippled
the mainspring of her neck
to ease up to my estuary door
in one shout of blood.
It's not so much a house
more a glass-bottomed ship
capsized and used as a house.
Or a minke whale with windows
basking on wet sand,
or a driftwood palace
on a royal mile of seaweed,
or a happening waiting an axe.
Its cracks are in the ocean's wax-free ear,
she says. She says
the grains of its waving wood
summon the tides.
I bottle her in the porch.
I garden her,
snipping the pulse of her wet vine.

SEA VIEWS

when I was young the suckling sea
moved about me
played on my limbs like reeds

in my teens the probing oceans
shrank to pools
tamed by easy swimming motions

in middle years I sat in shallows
dredging moats
the tide soon swallows

now I'm as old as pebble-stones
waves beat me
up, and stoke my bones

WITH A NOD TO BEACHY HEAD

for a Victorian Naturalist, Hawkshore, who found evidence that chalk
cliffs are undermined by limpets. His work was only recently validated

Flint blunts the ploughshare.
The damage isn't caused by storms.
Yet the village blacksmith knew his forge
must one day tumble from the cliff
and bellow down the ocean gorge.
And he knew

the marvel of trails etched
in iron rock, seen the living culprit,
learnt its name: Patella vulgata.
He asked a Science man, "Hawkshore,
what might limpets do
to chalk?"

They weighed the tell-tale calcium
from digestive tracts. Who'd foretell
the Science community
would retreat into a shell
in face of facts?
The truth is

who has the sharpest tongue?
the blacksmith asked the foundry-lad.
The plough? The sea? The limpet snail?
Unkind man, he'd say. Sad
mankind has the sharpest tongue
mark you me.

Invisible within her shell
the limpet licked and quarried.
In Nineteen Three the forge
went down to wind and frost and wave.
Science hammered on, unworried
in its cave.

SPIRIT OF BOSCASTLE

a found poem -

a new plaque on a riverside shop-front

Clovelly Clothing
destroyed by floods 16th August 2004
rebuilt 16th August 2004

BANDSTAND

Scratched on its drum skin
of albescent paint
the highlighted lows:

the sandstorm in effigy
the mid-season bake
the flute of a crashing claw.

On thirsting flooring boards
the elongated scuff
where the bandmaster turned

on practice nights,
and the shallow shiny indent
created by the cello rest.

Among night-scents
of shell-weed and sun shield
the polished applause of the sea

THE LAST RESORT

- Glifada, Corfu

They say the caterpillar tractors
came from landing craft. No-one saw.
And all the shapely thigh of hill
was shaved of Aleppo and Black pine
in a single night. The drivers fell
drugged by the resin, they say.

One year ago you would have looked
at olive, oak, the cypress, the carob
of the brae, rearranged softly
year-on-year in natural regeneration.
And the whispering white poplars
told of no settlement by man.
You would see the orange speckled clan
of salamanders taking early sun,
the plane tree near the stream,
the tree-of-heaven palm
in curved cascade between
          the darkness and the day.

Ulysses, shipwrecked on this sand
slept in his own arms. Here he saw,
in a porpoise's eye, the Atlantic sunrise
filtered through Herculean slabs
of Africa and Spain, liquefying gold
from a stadium of skies.

Sternbergia still reflects the sun's niche -
its low yellow flowers are a sealed knot.
But I miss the white petals of the sea squill
on a high September stalk, their multi-level
perfume, and their gentle way
with hours of storm, and hours of still.

TRICK OF LIGHT

the boathouse, brimmed among the trees
fails to register

whatever it's about
the rust-rilled roof
can't be an inlet of the sea
so you stay convinced of a dusty privacy
from which a face might peer or disappear

yet fisherboats crawl
downtide and catch fleetness of rig-line
in web-wet glass
and recognise their own
immediately

LEOPARD COVE

Through brambles, on the path to the sea
a wind-whipped figure
smaller than life, picks the finest berries

from inside the bush, working a circle,
surrounded by canes.
No obvious gap in the thorns, no exit.

"I'm waiting," he says, "waiting for the
ambient light
to improve." He waves grandly skyward.

Brand new sunlight breaks against his hands.
Awe-struck
I raise a quiet camera. "Not as good as mine,

my old friend." He heaves an ancient 'Agfa',

from the rucks of a sack,
"Smile for the finches."

On my stroll back, he's on a low sea-crag
designed for puffins.
He takes a single slow snap of the beach.

We're all in it.

SCOTLAND THE BRAVE

His tongue, claustrophobic
came out continually for Scotland
unco gallus (extremely reckless)

flesh off his back in Perth
red hair for a mattress
his Highland cow salted in The Lowlands

sty'd him with a pig, they did
in the brig of a schooner, bone rations
quartermaster halved

found Newfoundland
summer-shy sub-soil
north inscribed in glaciers

hairsted his fingernails, cockroach
henroach, any bliddy roach
sucked shavings, pined for home

To pricey Princes Street
the distant cousins now return
to trap wild shortbread

DOUBLE TAKE

at Breydon Water

You hear the pearl fall, the hollow tap
on the skimpy ice of the salt marsh.
You press keen eyes to the storm flap
as though in hope of a mating pair.

Where could the point of origin, be?
Your mind leaps to Oystercatcher –
the wader with the blooded beak.
Perhaps it dropped the lovely sphere

like a pit ejected by a blackbird.
Quick as a finch, you seize the pearl
and all at once you've manufactured
plans to pin it to your loved one.

But how did the treasure get here?
A feature of the Oystercatcher -
they never take, spear, or interfere
with oysters. What's in a name?

And then you hear bling bling -
an air taxi, hopping down the Yare –
an Essex girl - a broken string -
her tears torn from emptiness.

WHEN BONFIRES WERE GOLD

Trees were in fables.
Twigs were collectors' pieces.
Bony acre'd brassicas
ruled the peneplain of Thanet
where once were sweet oaks.
Bonfires - fruits

of the neap tide -
were strung along the bough shore
buttressed by decking
  from Rochester Rose -
the last sloop to land fish here.
Fertilised with fury

one stack grew, another shrank
to the tune of pram cars,
the acrid creak of pulleys,
high curses, and low prayers
for the speedy coming
of the Fifth.

The Third and Fourth
were respites. The sea swithered.
Nothing stalked along the sand.
An odd wand settled.
An odd crab.
The Moon.

BEFORE THE STORM

A perfectly ordinary August 1588 storm sank a
Spanish Armada whose seafarers were unused to
the rough ways of the North Atlantic. The same
equinoctial tempest swept away all last traces of the
Lancashire village of Singleton.

The Nereids wept at Queen Mary's death
and the Rossall coast stayed weal
but they shook their spurs at Elizabeth
and saltmarsh took the field.

                                      No more
the springing spikes of barley, rye, and oat.
Neptune wets the wattle, sucks the daub -
our cottage swims like a breached boat.
My grandfather sits and can't absorb.

Only Penny Stone Inn near Carlon -
the dozing megalith, her Colts Ring
and the hollow-eyed oaks of Singleton
stand proud.

                          I saw a kale wagon swing
like a galleass, sink below the mere,
drown father and son, and dogs beside
and the good horse, breaking traces, rear
like a stranded hippocampus, die.

TWIN SET

Knit one, purl one, drop one -
you pulled him back to make me.
He was russet and scarlet.
I'm scarlet and russet.
How I wish he could come round for tea.

If only you'd knit two together
it would be more Fair Isle, you see.
Though I am Arran
I'd feel so less barren
with a twin soul for company.

We share the same double stitch -
but he was cast off so young.
Both lanolin rich.
Both itching to itch.
If only you hadn't dropped one.

Please pull me back and make him -
his old splendour restore.
Let scarlet and russet
be russet and scarlet –
oh please run him up once more.

We will wander the Fair Isle
together, the two of us, him and me.
Comrades in arm
we'll adopt a sheep farm.
What a future for us there will be.

COME DAY CROW DAY

It's a day when hyper-frost and anti-freeze
argue as to what will cool the pistons.
Is our journey necessary? Much as any are,
replies the cheap upholstery. And maybe not,
chimes a broken roll-bar. Into ghost country,
the side country, the deserted ancestors.
At the curve's tongue, the badger's public grave
has fresh bloodmarks. A crow lops the air,
bells the frozen cow parsley, and storms
an upward arc denying the power of storm.
The sun's coin spins through winter larch
and, at the moment that we re-emerge,
the cuddling gale lets go the bodywork
and turns us pale.

THE PRIZE

A trim hedge points to a bald village.
Sodium glow creeps unwarranted
along the breastworks of a ditch.
A chaffinch nest, pierced, rubbished,
lays on the desolate brim of the road.
All of a parcel with the modern rage

for chain-saw management of hedgerows
to ease the Grand Guignol rampage
of the car. The villagers arrive for Easter,
swerve to avoid the tumulus nest.
A polecat moon paws-back the cloud's edge,
looks in. One fledgling left, on tiptoes,

cries in shorthand. No replies.
The cuckoo village quietens as it squats.
Day by day, carefully sewn moss, roots, grass
unwind, buffeted by cars that shuttle past.
A figure sweeps the parking lots.
Today's 'The Best Kept Village' prize.

PENDLE HERITAGE

The house has an old photograph. Lime frost on warm stone.
Bleached sap of blinds. His daedal moustache.
Her walled simplicity. And a grey scarf of light
The ginger cat wove.

A man close to death leans. A boy, given a game of statues,
Leaks naughtiness from dry corners of his mouth.
Others are embarrassingly ready, hot swaying currents,
Waiting for the little bird.

Marigolds loaf around in tubs. Iced smiles
And Victoria cake wait the servant's knife.
Crinoline and taffeta rumple in the sun. The faces crane out
A semitone darker than clouds.

They're near the cruck barn. See the remnants of string
Decaying even then. One man moves. The bridegroom?
The skull of a skidding horse cracks against the wall stud.
Rude lightning

Heard in a coma. The yowl of gudgeon pins,
The ghosts winnowed naked on the threshing floor,
The cry of the oak forest spun from the Druid's hand
By the tide.

IN THE CHEQUERED ZONE

He's here because he's here, you know.
Sightseers come to stake their claim
as though reviewing next door's fence,
their minds on Hammersmith's traffic flow,
or Saturday's big promotion game,
the air of terror – price of vigilance.
May he tug their sleeve before they go
to ask, Did General Wyatt know my name
left blank for your Remembrance?

The ancient abbey knows full well
about the young misunderstood.
But the church is dumb, except its bell
and a mum saying, Sorry for my brood.
Peace - being too long stabled with the dead -
something dramatic ought to happen here
at this fallen envelope of stone
perimeter'd with weary poppy feet -
The Angel of Mons perhaps appear.
Or the man himself, promoted pawn
of the sacrifice, dying to be the decent-
minded youth who'd murder a beer
and, shot of this musty chequered zone,
enjoy an hour of footie in the street.

And so we shuffle blankly out
spent as cartridges. Big Ben bound
we steel ourselves for one more shout
at seeing London in the round -
its peace campaign on the roundabout.

MOUNTAIN STARS

a terza rima
stars, invisible by day
- Longfellow

Longfellow saw no stars by day
but wasn't short of them at night.
Streetglow masks our Milky Way.

Okay, Serpent-Bearer copped a bite
and died - risky occupation.
But Orion's hound is seriously quiet.
The Great Bear needs a helping hand.
Castor, Pollux, have gone west.
The Water Bearer's drowned.

You lucky mountaineer, blessed
with all the star-groups. Only Swan,
Eagle, Lyre, still shine
                 for us off-Everest.
And when the last constellation's gone
I'll be reaching for a piton.

HOW DO I LOOK?

In a mirror, the world's at peace
with itself. Till we interfere.
Why can't we look. And just be us!
In a mirror, the world's at peace
with itself. Till we interfere.
We pose, strut, so never release
that certain look that says 'sincere'.
In a mirror, the world's at peace
with itself. Till we interfere.

HIGH CULTURE

The ability to talk to Alpine flowers
falls flat at apres-ski.
So I save my chat, and climb for hours
on the goat path, free

to walk, to talk to the Annuals
in the sunlit Pass at dawn,
by noon be conversational
with Gentians on The Matterhorn.

Much depends on genus and altitude.
Heliacrysum stays schtum.
Saxifraga's always rather mute -
like talking to a kitchen broom.

But when I reach the summit ice
there's a voice both white and breezy.
Edelweiss, Edelweiss,
every morning she greets me.

UNDER WRAPS

Through a misted slop-house window
The Moon shied itself at me so it did,
a thin pockmarked pizza, heavy on salami,
saying there's more might hit the eye:
a micro-meteorite might, so fast you'd miss it.
I'm sure those Venn Diagram craters
on the dry Passchendaele Moon
feature in some magazine's pattern of dahlias
for a scatter-cushion. So rest easy.

Ha! Adams and Eves of expelled rock
touching themselves to sleep are just
embroidery hoops. We've had fifty million
years of polite, quiet, creation;
just forty thousand tonnes of space-debris
each year. Routine as piercing a drum.
Corky moonlight floats on rose cloud.
All's well. No dark side of the fabric;
It's all sewn tight as a telescope case.
Put your eye close. Mind the odd needle.

GABARDINE HUNT OF THE SUN

I surf the simmering charity shops
for something gabardine.

With padlocked nose and croupier's hand
I screw my eyes, go sight unseen

through tacky camel hair, fatiscent leather,
suave anorak, wiggle-wick of astrakhan

that feels it could be desiccated brain
collared from The Upper Amazon.

Ritz and plain, plain, ritz, ritz and plain
a true democracy of shared stain,

of shoulder-rub, of 'all equal on the rail'.
Pity I'm never doing this again...

Ah!.... the worsted pull of gabardine.
I pay. I go. And feel mean.

BLESSED-FAIR SONNET

.....what's so blessed-fair that fears no blot?
-Shakespeare Sonnet 92

*'The Sun' newspaper erased the image of a handicapped girl who
had been invited, with her father, to join the team photograph of
the England Cricket Team. The public outcry brought changes for
the better in photo-journalism.*

*Merope: the Greek goddess who fell in love with a man and was
punished by being made over as an invisible star in the sky.*

Her father proud as Atlas, rounding off the row.
Wheelchair and crouching fielders at the front,
the two honoured guests smiling. Oh I should say so.
A fine gesture this. Loyal fans. For an instant
all the team's white strength and theirs, a continent,
a beaming family in a host of The Pleiadean stars.
How do we view the tabloid's digital affront
airbrushing her kind face and painting a colapsar?
Who loused things up? Who made her disappear?
Who now remembers Merope, whose immortality
has died for love and whose image is a dark star?
Technology can wipe any soul. Spoil any party.
We are all daughters of Pleione, waiting in line
for the brush-off. None may fit The Grand Design.

MOON DAY

One of those ambiguous days
when the moon hangs out in the sun
and Venus is lit by a festive bulb
as you queue at the stop for town.

The full day moon is a shop-girl
you're shocked to see, from the bus,
ghost through defensive walls
like ice on a winter moustache.

The single ticket is pale and rich
twice doubled with lilac shadow.
Cats' eyes wink on the river.
The roads are blind with snow.

Signing you off on your own -
the moon, like a keeping sister,
burns her face on your cheeks,
grips your hand briefly in hers

and, for once, the world seems
ringingly transparent.
People even smile a little
as if something mattered.

But, repentant flea, the moon
returns to her old narrow stall
the supermarket giant sun
will dominate tomorrow.

THE POETRY SHED

Two degrees to starboard
in ten years - its wood coat
stagey as a dose of cardboard
eternal as a longboat.

Kids respect its drum calls
its spiders (wide as jam lids).
Kids don't hit the shed with balls
or pry away the whippy ribs.

As earwigs in a house-of-cards
the tenants come, the tenants go
Over the door, a diamond star
embellishes the patio.

The shed strains to almost fit
the pitted spade, encrusted rag
sleeping hyacinth, fig biscuit
earth-scented carpetbag,

squirreled offcuts, knotted wire
rusty horticultural floss
fungal-penetrated coir
tottery vases, better lost.

HEALED BY A WORD

I'm pulled up short by Philip Larkin's feel
for words. He deployed the verb to cicatrize
conveying, skin over, mark with scars, to heal.
I am ill at this time, sick enough to fully prize
this word I met – the tender point of origin
on a living stem where a leaf said goodbye.
Will the word stretch to the maculate skin
near a lager lout's lapidated eye?
Maybe. For tired Larkin, enough to recall
when words tore his innards; sombre journal
entries, blanker, echo a leaf's dying fall.
Decision time. I reach for that infernal
cicatrize. Do I have the everlasting gall
to contemplate deploying the word at all?

THE CHEMISTRY BETWEEN

A Chemistry lab of a certain age
is a hot house of spillingly catchy odours
subliming, from each benchtop stain
and reservoir crack, to stiffen the nose.
Tiny effusive reactions fizzle and rise,
burn, unbutton, breed, embrace
in a random menagerie that commonly thrives
unremarked but for the wizard smell of the place:
cabbage disulphide, bad egg sulphide,
the cordial ripeness of pear and gas,
and methyl hydroxy benzaldehide
(vanilla essence a cake knows it as).
From this random house might emerge
the everything cure, or the ultimate scourge.

THINKING IT A TOY

A blood-red little chest expands
on the window's outer shell.
One jaw of hell, or a carnival carnation?
I like the radio alarm to mark time.
I like to sleep in the depths of a dream cruise
and wake with a steam-hammer near my cell.
At one remove, I take in half the news most of the time.
This one day I trilled against the shell of sleep
and heard 'The Today Programme'
through a crack.... thinking it a toy...
Now, what might innocence mistake and use?
Empty can of cola? Mobile 'phone?
Think Angola. Pin of a tractor-trailer?

They thought it was a toy. The landmine exploded
on the kitchen floor. Three boys died.
Their sister's hands were severed.
Graffiti-fresh, the children call out in the dark
first morning of the holidays.

TALKING THROUGH THE TOP OF A GLASS HAT

"Words are stained glass
held in place by leaden quiet."
Who said that? Don't know
but I'll buy it.

I want to shake out the glass,
transfer the stains
to paper. So I write,

"The red pane..." But the words
bear only the weight of: traffic-light,
brothel, hairline fracture of the brain.

I need the language of stain:
what copper oxide
can say that no poet can.
Surely William Morris, Burne-Jones
know. They blush and go.

The glass-blowers fill
my tea-break.
"Words don't glow, mate.
Glass can't speak.
Mostly, when you see 'red', it's not,
not really, is it?
But red glass,
now that's pure red."

THE BIRTH OF A SPOON

He has a car mechanic's hands, but stronger.
Delicate crafts have built the skeletal muscle
in tense harmonies of elastic band
wrapped on twin steel bobbins. He works longer
hours than anyone, gives no-one any hassle.
At home he keeps to his work-bench land
of jewellers' pliers, tweezers, warm seltzer.
New born silver spoons, quaintly thistled,
are his raw material. Contraband.

Glasgow via Freemantle, in a cosy cot
of bubble plastic. He snatches one up,
and for two days this will be his precious lot.
He'll Cloisonné it rich as a Tsar's cup,
as mazed with secrets as a microdot.

Back to his cover on rainy Monday
in the industrial stomach of Newcastle,
marking his card at Breecher's Garage,
gouging the crankshaft out of a Mini.
There's a node of his mind, a citadel
graced by enamel pools, Cobalt and beige,
in the lamp-lit black of the car bay.
One day there'll be a car that won't rattle,
he anticipates. They'll be all the rage,
for ever. Incorruptible, once got.
He gives the seized axle one more larrup
with a mole wrench. No more damned rot,
and rust. He'll build a real rival to the galloped
horse, and feel its muscles flex and knot.

THE OPAQUE SPIRIT

Kingsgate Castle in Thanet

A robin's microsecond of alarm
starts my mental clock
pulls my gaze up lines of turret windows.
And on the wall are many works of art.
There's a spirit in each flint's rain-black pupil
set proud in its mortar iris.
And, seen from such distance
as lovers use for stringing kisses,
faint as mermaid-memories of dryness,
swimming in stone
are the simplified silica bones
of ancient sponges
squeezed dry by the potter.
There's the shy wink of unbroken pebble
as the gallery recedes.
With as many faces as the sea
the stones ripple in the sun.

SACRED MIRROR

At the back of the beach
the Naiku – the inner shrine -

unkempt, fussy or formal,
loud, proud, Art Nouveau, banal

exterior plywood, Swedish pine
tongued-and-grooved

in studious line abreast -
iterations of shabby-genteel

hyperborean chambers
Apollo's lost followers

marshalled as caves of desire
when they outgrew the tide -

a long parliament
inhaling the gloss and the sand flea

giving the elbow to all man-made
except for a kettle, a cup

and a child's tiny spade.

TELEGRAM

DR. ELSA HAHN. AGE 35. ARRIVING HOVE 14.7.63. STOP.

Well, she came she sawed she chuntered on
with eminent authority:
a smiling doting blond Shakespeare Companion.

Or outside you could hear Brighton Beach
as the clenching pebble faces clattered
in a fusion of keys. Intimate. Out of reach.

She summed up King Lear: a paradigm
of Unaccomodated Man? Pity
a corroded life, yes. But the lesson

was lost on me. Doctor, if you do not write, you leech.
How do you know what mattered
in the over-reaching of a king. And creature

comfort? Have you survived when hope had gone?
Hardly! I went with no temerity
after-hours, Dear Doc., where is your qualification
for understanding pain? Her blue eyes beseeched.

She rolled a sleeve. Slate-
fresh, a black inlay on her peach

skin; 4 2 6 9 1 5 3 1.....Belsen.

MARY YOUNG

died 13 Oct 1939 aged 91,
Lowgill, Bentham

What perfume came at the last, Mary Young?
Did springtime steep your frail bed
with spirituous buttercup, spring sedge,
rare agrimony, resonant pine
that final autumn?

What did you see at the last, Mary Young?
The Wellsian plumes of the bombing range?
Or Mill Bridge – where your girl's hand had composed
a tower of ekstatic pebbles
entablatured by sun?

What did you hear at the last, Mary Young?
The drone of a storm at the sheepfold gate,
the leaves turning turtle, artillery
at Wennington?

What did you think at the last, Mary Young?
That your world was tipping back
like mine, in a Ford Pilot car
on the slope of a river pontoon,
when the rusted hand-brake-cable broke
and the sky swung?

What did you cling to at last, Mary Young?
I grabbed for my Mum. Competent Dad
put his foot down - the family
was saved. Did you reach out
to Lowgill's Good Shepherd
to take you home, Mary Young?

THE KNAVE'S GRAVE

From early Norman days – the grave of Jeppe Curteys

The village awards boundary burials
to its wilder sons – the cutpurse,
the heister of hoards, the breaker of styles,
the coin clipper, sheep raper, worse.
Some have bushels of stones to stay them;
the very few, like Jeppe - a grave stan.
The elders, with a guilty pride then,
keep Jeppe at the hub of three hams:
Pendleton, Sabden, and wise Wiswell
and, walking between, they'll greet
the thieving spell of Mister Jeppe -
the outsider - taken to the secret heart
of the old vibrant village web.
They have him, like their old religion,
to serve a higher purpose after death.

THE MASON'S BRACKET

- Gloucester Cathedral

Apprentices memorialised in stone
are rare as epitaphs on traffic cones

and this young mason's death-fall
from the high vault to the choir stall

rings a curiously futuristic bell.
Just out of reach, the monumental L

of a mason's square carved in stone
could be solar panels, a space station.

Launched from the vault's shaft
the poor boy, strange craft,

free-falls in outstretched desperation
as a helpless crew look on.

I resume my cool summer stroll
impacting on the dark cathedral

more reverently. The souvenirs.
The café. Porchway. Stars.

VAN GOGH WAS HERE...

*......and is said to have been inspired, in his later and revolutionary
use of colour, by an exceptional play of light over the sea,
viewed from The East Cliff in Ramsgate.*

Forever 'Orchard', or 'Sunflowers'
or 'A Plain near Auvers',
in fashion, out, ambient as June showers.

He stood on this cliff once; Finisterre
darkened, fine chalk dust blew the sea
a mineral blossom, sweet as pear.
Ocean had that yellow hue, last seen
in childhood, through facets of a vase
one summer on The Wadden Zee.

I'm here, attracted to the dodgem cars
vying bib-to-bib like famished gulls.
The grey-green sea holds no hurrahs.
To think, La Manche, today as dull as
this, gifted Vincent all his colours.

MAPS

Unfolding a map is a joy to me –
a minimum shake and the sheet cascades.
To avoid the reverse origami
I leave charts around, not quite displayed.
I winter-finger-walk my way round
these close-imagined, clean, green and trim
utopias. My maps are a godown
of never-tried-ways, corks from a hat-brim
dancing, just out of reach of surprise.

Title, continuity, border, scale, key,
all point to an academy, sage, wise
that oversees human geography.
But all maps encourage restlessness.
In opening one, I am dispossessed.

THE PALM HOUSE OF THE FIVE WINDS, HAIFA

Below the cooling forest of Mount Carmel
the city boils. High tech hums away on web sites, in bars,
on secret balconies. Haifa gloats as her balustrades unravel
through shopping glass, into the arms of her sometime lover
The Mediterranean Sea. A brass-necked temptress,
she sits best on a golden cushion, defying Napoleon
but welcoming all prophets and builders of follies.
Especially from London. So what if the palm house might say,
"Queen Victoria burnt her skirts here leaving hoops of iron,"
should it not reflect an empire of madness dressed as action?
Lawrence of Arabia gave a full Tremadog laugh
at the greenhouse without glass. What it is to be sane.

Who can say? It has a French feel. Incomplete.
Magnificent. The maximum use of infrequent rain.

SLOE TRAIN

slow sloe train
well-named, pauses often,
often nowhere near a station
often to let roads through
or cattle, or fox to safe haven

or give a lift to a rambler
who looks a touch tired
just for conversation
with one of the five guards
or vacationing signalmen
who enjoy the train's pace
or visit the driver's daughter
who ties her blouse on sticks
to flag us down

or cool our feet in the river's
murmuring tones
or write poems about sloe
liqueur (made with gin
in a still on the slow sloe train)

PISUM SONG

I had an early love affair with fresh peas

the way they pulled
at the bridge of my thumb
to burst forth on the mission
of parched rowers

with all but the last, the little cox, eased
in the narrow stern
saying, done the job, kept them trim
till harvested
stemmed the worst of their ambition

A WORD TO THE UNWISE

Who gave the name of 'rape' to the dainty oil-seed?
Rapum, Latin word for turnip. Why mislead?

Lucus, Latin for the woodland shade,
came to mean the obverse: 'light', instead.
So lucus a non lucendo is a word-made-paradox,
a knowing word, a deceitful etymon, a fox
in hounds' clothing with a double-cross in each eye.
He takes his alter ego everywhere. As an alibi.

In the pseudonymity of 'English Public School'
'Public' doesn't play the game at all.
Public? Oh come on! But the derivation
of the name reveals, like Briar Fox, its true bacon.
The sense of 'Public', intended by its eponym,

pricks old-boys to public service. The antonym,
'private', leaps to attention in this more democratic age
whereas, before, it must have fallen through the page,
the rich were raised so far above the poor.

BEARDED

At the Bearded Theory family music festival in 2009, Ashbourne,
Derbyshire, the main stage was upturned by a mini tornado.

Technicians tweak the inna velvet
earthquake amps to the Armaggedon mark.
The microphone rises, the music stage flips
like a carton of eggs clawed by a cat.
Grownups huddle – chicks on a chimneystack.
Youngsters chase papers – just loving it.

The skylark sweep of the farmer's meadow
has arranged a buckshee centrepiece
- a twister, unlisted on the programme page.
Children rise in the air in comic slowmo
to be clutched away in gleeful ruckus.
From earth in the field, they soon emerge

to slap a collage, design a bath-ball,
kick-box the lunging walls of the site,
dance conga with face-painter Donna Mckay,
till thoughts re-ascend in a scrambling tangle
of tailing line from a cavernous kite,
no surely a tent, setting sail in the ruby sky.

A staid marquee, with stanchions that work,
sings through a larynx of steel guys,
and lifts its skirts as pantomime wings
revealing Joanna who treats folk for shock.
Intent in their own swaying bay, kiddies
all beards and bows and rainbow fingers

are yearning to tumble again over Kansas.
But brandy from Jo brings the elders back
with hackles raised and shackling hands
to haul them off. See! Men on stretchers!
Look how the whirlybird lifts them, dark
on the stars. Bet those guys had other plans.

FRANKINCENSE

The store had a tray of samplers
with wild names, alphabetically in bottles
to instill an air of discipline.

One label promised frankincense.
Frank: from frankus – free, unconstrained.
And on this particular day

the noses of passers-by
had stripped the spirit from its oriental well
of limited sanctuary.

Please let there be more.
The shop assistant livened. "Go", she advised,
"and crush wild marjoram by hand.

Light a fire of pinewood.
Let the fragrances combine. Notice, the common
and the very rare are similar

how a native woodland
can provide as close an evocation of divinity
as Rome found in Arabia."

Then she fell back on
herself, went off among her lonely manicure
shaking a fingernail to dry.

SHOPPING FOR ENGLAND

She rides the Harrod's lift all day
between Ground and Fourth, this au pair,
a return ticket, pinned
to grandmother's bodice
loose as tug-smoke on her.

She's hitched from Gdansk to research
"social interaction in English elevators".
We lambs, of course, are silent
sealed, undelivered.
She stands, perseveres

but her audio machine runs mute, runs
deep in cable noise. Our solemn faces
have been riveted in place.
This harbour is too small
to risk collision

so each soul rides its petty little anchor.
Disappointed in her hosts,
the opening of doors
takes on a fascination

THE BODY OF WORK

I had a desk, or so I fondly thought
beneath junk mail, junk writings, junk.
But when one Spring I cleared my lines
to make work for the dustcart
there was no bureau there. Nor trunk.
Just computer paper stacks, and bacon rind
dating back, in green and greener rings
to the original nursery floor
where I first chewed and scribbled things.
I sighed, and bought a desk and drawer.

VESTIGE

Evolution's vestige of a tail
in us, the coccyx,
is Greek for 'cuckoo';
the prism of bone recalls a bird's beak.
And there it sits, permanent as chain-mail
surviving by tricks:
a last drop of dew
turned to diamond, one last tweak

of life between the cheeks, a Braille
memory of the sticks,
the wider zoo
when we weren't atrophied and weak.

HOLY AT HOME

for Giovanni Malito

I'd intended the full monty: supper,
naked, pure, stripped from the back-lot.
I'd minted new spuds with ginger mint,
broadly buttered beans, slivered parsnip;
table-knifed them in a mound.

And at my right hand, green
as Gethsemane, the salad bowl gloated
bird-like on my stainless fork. This. Whole.
Fresh. Food. But, even as I spoke,
the cells broke.

Each meal a sharp
intake of death. We are what we batten upon:
the worm, apple: the sparrow-hawk, sparrow:
The whale is a monument to plankton:
the termite, carved

in ebony. And we
we are all of the above. Only Death,
hologram table-mats, antique pepper-mills,
embossed silverware, survive
to clatter past

the head-waiter.
Bric-a-brac evades the pyre.
No shortage of young guns aiming to be
patrons of the table we'd prized
and set aside as ours.

My mouthing soul
casts round for bread: Bread
that perisheth not. (Though 'perisheth'
has perished in its turn.)
Only The Last Supper

lasts.

THE SLEEPING WALK TO PELEKAS

Hostel rooms don't boast, but this one did,
lit by the cool sunroof of a rainbow.
Its tin beds, chariots of sublimating peace.
A room of cantilevered kindness, rid
of sock stench by pink cyclamen. A show home
to grab the dropped out, a new lease
on death for remembered bourgeois guile.
A light sun-dried glimpse of caged doves
released my soul on strings above tile
skies. I slept, adrift from past loves.

The Old Quarter of Corfu Town confounds
the day-glow tourist, hides behind washing
on spicery balustrades. Ink-jet welling
shadows fuse across the cobbles. No sounds
can stir. But in my dream the 'English Swing',
Venetian smock, and loud French dressing,
all put on a single face. A Greek mask. Unmanned
by sin and sun. A visage dipped in cricketing lore,
Yorkshire tea, and the pomp of a good brass band.
Was that him, hanging or banging a door?

Pale as a jailer, hung on varicose arms,
a crucified horse, installed between
one tubular bed and its twin brother?
His familiar voice, born to be bellicose,
bore a youth hostel warden's Ryvita-clean
humour, packing lunch, talking weather.
The 'spearers of game' would not smooch girls
around here. We rested assured. Booted
against the abrasive limestone foothills,
we trekked the oleanders' line to Alepou.

No-one invested with life can resist
this fourteen kilometre hike. Pelekas.
It hauls out your prestigious mind, grey
on the pumice, dead, and never once missed.
The body's a living cell of the land. Because
of autumn's glut, plum, walnut, grape, all day
spill to hand, in the fields near Kokini's well.
If prickly pear spines tear my page to dust
the poem will write itself on air, and carousel
to the speedy swallows' dry mud nest.

FLOWER OF CHIVALRY

they reached lower

as children might
on the river
for a pinprick flower

a young knight
albata armoured
and his lover

and he fell
he gravitated over

no fight
no play of martyr

soon, albedo
reigned once more

to cover
all but his last word
"Forget-me-not"

which lives
and is the flower

JUDITH

I took her in as naturally
as milk absorbs wild honey
she who shunned the blood of cattle

even in the desert of my war
a certain discipline
her mind a hive of industry

and kohl black eyes
passionate, Godly, grateful.
More than self sufficient

with her wallet of wine
her parched smuggled corn
and her mild request

for licence
to bathe in Bethulia's fountain
under the chaste stars

My affections followed her
as oil of yellow jasmine
trails a pollen bee

and on the fourth night
I shut my military swarms away
placed her at my bosom

and surrendered
to a better general, one with a taste
for the jugular

A LOWRY

- for my dentist with his copy of a painting
by L.S. Lowry titled
'A Lancashire Village 1937'

I lean toward the Lowry.
Suits a waiting room, a busy print.
Something to scrutinise before one dies.
I fumble feebly after specs. I squint.
See that lass, no bigger than a loaded brush
her laughter buried in a bowler hat,
who ignores the Friday homeward rush
subsumes the darkness like a cat?
Her shade will share my slow descent.
While Novocaine invades the gum,
my soul will croon her merriment:
on wishbone legs I will be young.

Ach, the Monday mill begins to shout,
Finished. Sit up. Rinse. Spit out.

THE FUNERAL OF MY AUNT

a sassy lady, slender, strong,
liable to goose the parson, duck the sermon -
or deliver one of her own

you never conformed
to old age, always found that souls
needed a naughty whisper or a good shake

and headstones only tempted you to hurdle
or sit against and read a racy book
or watch the plain sailing butterflies

but it wasn't a tedious service -
and all the diaspora family came
to say how you would have warmed

to the children, new to any church,
who echo-found the bell tower
with summer giggles

to the bluebird fountain of weeping irises
the fluttering hush of candles
and those hats to die for

THE PASSING ON OF HATS

You had this thing for millinery
or, rather, didn't. Didn't care
what lidded you. If it were columnar
your high object was achieved.
Or if it were a scarlet flare
with corky grapes. Or feather starred
fox jaws. Or bandoleer'd in finery.
You simply sent your best pin
wrestling the mirror. "Lah-di-dah"
you'd say, "Baroness Muck," then
sail off to town, in that ladyship way
to net another specimen.

I rummage in the attic. Can't say
where they all have gone.

THE PASSING OF A PIPE

A brier pipe -
   POW style
chiselled with phlegm and scissor.
Sanded with paste of Calvados and wood-ash.
Bored by liberated nailfile.
Hollowed by native woodlice.
And smoothed by your good hand -
carved you a coffin in a while.

Somewhere on Tobacco Road
among the wild rose and sundew
there'll be a shrine to cold
warriors who thought they knew
that to survive meant heavily to smoke.

NEEDLE

piercing a floral
sampler of laid-work, ready
as the day she went -
    her only will and testament

I squint through the blunt eye,
recall her

    skirmishing with cotton lengths
parched lips, back bent
ever composing herself
to find
    the argumentative thread's end

in permanent red with the rent
she sewed
for what amounted to,
    at best, a few drab pence

the needle is my mother's monument

TOO YOUNG TO FORGET

Come here, lad, I'm going to pin it on you.
Red for blood, black where the bullet's in.

Why would I want a bullet hole reminding
her of death? I hadn't had my living yet.
But I gave in. Rules of the asylum.
The flat waving fields wore them. So must I.

She showed me a sketch drawn
by Grandad, keeping his head low.
Distant windmill, two trees, a dusky river.
On white card then. Or yellow.

Tithed memories. All I had of him
has crumbled into beige chalk dust.
You see, I took the picture from its frame
as children do, as children must.

As war churned the landscape
he drew it back to life again. Somme Horizon.
Calm rye grass. No poppies. I walked
the long line, looking for him.

MENIN BLACK

He's felt the apologetic lurch
with which a plough
unearths a high explosive shell

but in a corner of a foreign field
that is forever dangerous
Luk shrugs, finishes the furrow.

He damps down the engine,
walks the long stir
of turned ground and bullish gulls.

He pauses, studies, frowns, turns
toward his rig,
at peace among the milling birds.

He pours coffee, unfolds breakfast
on a gingham towel.
Crisp dark bread. Sweet tomato

and today's gift from the hive.
His wide hands
cradle a muddied mobile phone.

He wipes it quiet, shields his eyes.
A NATO plane
glides between Armentieres

and the careless-lidded honey
of landscape
slowly finding its ancient level.

I'LL WAIT HERE

The dizzy iron of the gate
is drunk on snowdrop wine.
Tansy blurs the capstones
of the high retaining wall.
I straighten my clothes,
undress my senses, prepare to be
the cloud-wide courtyard
sprung with pools and sharp reflected smiles.
Mark my hours with terracotta urns
of rhizomes, and let me be the glad sleep
of bamboos, ferns and variegated grasses.
When Spring comes:
each second a primrose,
each minute a pale daffodil.
And when the twelve hours are done
it will be summer.

FUNERARY RONDEL

- or why I wore a yellow suit to your funeral

Anne Boleyn wore yellow
to mourn for Catherine.

On with my dickey-bow
(dismal black's always in)
but why stifle all colours
elysian? Why ape crows?

Anne Boleyn wore yellow
to mourn for Catherine.
Hal sported white to go
and bury Anne Boleyn.

You liked men showy, so
I conformed to Anne, and
to mourn for Catherine
Anne Boleyn wore yellow.

THE YOUNG TOMB

In The Middle Ages everyone was old
any child will confirm that. But he was young, the Archbishop,
smooth of skin and stone.
No name tag intercedes for him with such as me.
But I feel the chisel on his bone,
know his weariness, how he holds himself closing up shop.
His voice is in the limestone, in the cave of his cathedral.

And who will be your be your master, now I am so ill?

The sculptor has the man relaxed at last, on a double pillow.
The wet lip. The flare of nostril. The trace of soft face-hair.
The spaniel's dry grief.

ST. BEDE THE VENERABLE

from a prayer of The Venerable Bede
delivered on the Feast of Saint Chad

"Christ washed their feet
and so will I.
No matter what post of
responsibility
they offer me, I rise no
higher than
to wipe their ankles dry."

And though, in the end
he had power
thrust upon him in - as
a dry thorn in the vow
of obedience -
warm was his water
smooth was his towel.

A VILLANELLE FOR BERNARD

Your power to engineer argument
might have made you a politician -
the village was quieter when you went -

but, solidarity with the poor, meant
piloting sewers – admirable mission.
Your power to engineer argument

had woken hearts. Take on the government!
You gave a fine "Red Flag" rendition.
The village was quieter when you went

to live in town, directing excrement.
Side-lined was your engine of sedition,
your power to engineer argument.

Thumping tubs had never paid your rent.
The pithead closed. And your position.
The village was quieter when you went.

A tinsel factory we've been sent
No one can moan, for no one's driven.

Your power to engineer argument!
The village was quieter when you went.

RED OCTOBER

Many have tried to breed a red budgerigar....

His daylight was a shed
where Arisaig smoke gave flight
to versicolour dreams.
When a crate of herring fell
on his metatarsal bones –
he fell back on Ardnish calm

and bred a budgerigar or two
or nine: Yellow Perihelion,
Grey Storm, Blue Larch,
Innocent Sam The White –
the names are in the breed book.
And when his heart stalled
and his soul prepared to fly
he came with cupped hands
to his bothy door, and willed

to the scattered world
Red October.

THE TREES ARE DOWN

- on helping to destroy an olive grove to make way
for new cotton fields

At harvest time the white rising air
of cotton fields draws the musk, of grapes
and ciderous apples, through the grove.
Today, deep in fallen olives, the labourers
question why the trees get no reprieve.

Sharpened by gloom, a farm boy climbs.
The branches weave their gentlest spell
like a dog with a violent master.
The bough stoops, begs for sanctuary:
each leaf with its own silver certainty.

The timber gives way.
We're showered with drupes of olives
and the venerable dust of old pollen.
The Dryads weep for this 'loss of balance'
which we carry everywhere; first we shout

then, in the same choking breath, we laugh
and leap like frogs among the fallen
limbs of wood, and pluck, with iron fingers,
warm olives to keep them from the fire.
Only the tree roots are staunch, till sprung

from the earth, uprooted by hydraulic digger.
A thousand years of quiet fertility
reduce to smoke in the gloaming air.
The breeze blows harder in the absence of the grove.
One by one the farm shutters close.

VILLAGE CELESTE

Roads quarter the common. Evening drags
at dimpled stone. Residual clock-hands
on the tower proclaim that it is midnight
or, if day, noon.

All is closed save the graveyard.
The stock of village life (the pub, the school,
the general store), hollow megaliths
among the solid ripeness of the corn.

Above a lodge a weathervane is bent
immobile, as if one sign of change
would summon Death, disturb the warden.
A window droops in ivy's dull mask.

The wine-cellar door is steeled with nails.
The famous kitchen garden, umber-lit
encroached by pines, shows only remnant
mutant cabbages, and dry cider-traps.

No meadows of tawny, tan and grey;
only standard gold, and modified rape
to come, and the grubbing-machine
in the long hedge of a child's laugh.

THE EVICTION

the long brocades of slumbering kale
meet at the cattle shieling ground
Dry washing bunts, tourniqueting
The tithe cottage is up for sale -

the talk in 'Little Queen' is all around
her going. But the clothes are hung again
The balefire yellow dress, dancing wassail
flags her staying to all the village round.

Irene clips, crazy-eyed, up the paving
The bailiff's men disturb a pheasant male
Their stiff boots talk of shootings down.
John Smith looks, then counts his pigs in

The glowering sky, the vanishings
meet at the distant cattle shieling ground
No house here. Just embers, quitting
the long brocades of slumbering kale